ARROW BOOK

SCIENCE FACTS

(Abridged)

(Original title: THE ANSWER BOOK)

By Mary Elting

*Illustrations by Tran Mawicke, John Ballantine,
Erwin Hoffman, William Bryant,
Stanley Polczak*

SCHOLASTIC BOOK SERVICES

Published by Scholastic Book Services, a division
of Scholastic Magazines, Inc., New York, N. Y.

CONTENTS

A question is one of the most useful things in the world. So is an answer. But no one ever needs to feel ashamed of saying, "I don't know." There are many things that even the greatest scientists have to admit they don't know—yet. The fun of answering really starts when you say, "I'm not sure, but let's see if we can find out."

—Mary Elting

I. TRAVELING INTO SPACE

Are other planets like the earth?

When the first explorers visit another planet they will certainly find it different from the earth. We don't know exactly what visitors might see on any of the planets, but here are some of the scientists' guesses.

Thick heavy clouds surround Venus. The planet's surface may be one great desert. Or it may be a landless ocean — or a vast jungle of strange plants that grow in spite of poison gases in the atmosphere.

Jupiter and Saturn also have cloudy atmospheres. Both planets are very cold. Neptune, Uranus and Pluto are even colder. Perhaps they have rivers of liquid air flowing among rocks of dry ice. Mercury, on the other hand, is very hot. Its rivers, if it has any, may be liquid metal flowing into metal seas.

A visitor to Mars would feel more at home. Mars probably has growing plants which change color with the seasons. Ice caps cover the north and south poles. Do animals live on Mars? Perhaps a camera in a spaceship may tell us before visitors land to see for themselves.

Gravity on Mars is less than on earth. It would be easy to take twenty-foot strides on Mars. But Jupiter's gravity would slow you down to a creep. There you would feel as if you weighed three times as much as you do on earth.

How does a rocket engine work?

You can make a kind of rocket engine. All you need is a toy balloon.

Blow air into the balloon. The more you blow the bigger it gets. That is because air inside it pushes hard against the thin rubber wall and stretches the balloon out, round and fat.

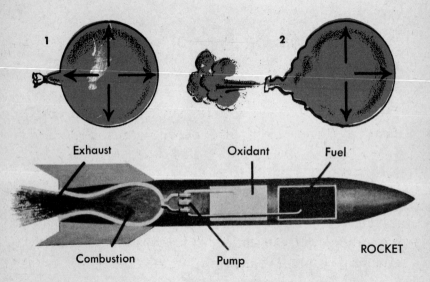

ROCKET

Now stop blowing. Let the balloon go. It will dart away from you with a whoosh. What makes it fly? Look at the pictures and you will see.

In the first picture the arrows show air pushing against the whole inside wall of the balloon. In the second picture the air at the back of the balloon has nothing to push against. It spurts out through the hole. But air at the front keeps on pushing. It pushes the whole balloon forward.

6

In a real rocket engine, fiery hot gases are made when the rocket's fuel burns. With a sudden roar the gases spurt out through a hole in the back. And at the same time, the gases are pushing at the front end, too. And this sends the rocket flying up and away.

Scientists have discovered that rockets work according to a rule. The rule says that any push in one direction causes an equal push in the other direction.

Is a jet engine the same as a rocket?

Look at the picture of a rocket and you will see how it gets its push forward. Fuel burning inside it makes the push. A jet engine gets its push in the same way. However, there is a difference between jets and rockets. A jet engine needs oxygen to burn its fuel, and it gets the oxygen from the air *outside*. A rocket carries *inside* itself everything it needs to make its fuel burn.

Now you can see why space ships must have rocket engines. A rocket can go far out into space where there is no air. It can keep running on its own supplies.

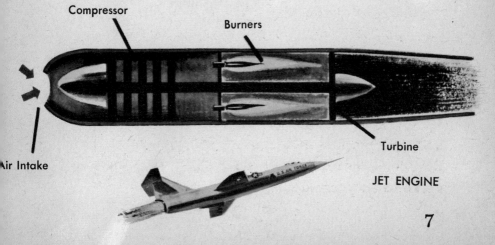

Compressor

Burners

Turbine

Air Intake

JET ENGINE

Why does a space rocket go so fast?

Up, up goes a rocket. Its powerful engines thrust it upward, fighting against the downward pull of earth's gravity. Higher, higher — the pull of gravity grows weaker. The rocket travels faster, faster. At last it is going 25,000 miles an hour. That is nearly seven miles a second. Such a blast of speed kicks the rocket beyond the place where gravity can slow it down enough to make it fall back to earth. The rocket has escaped! Now it can go coasting easily through space.

Does a rocket *have* to go so fast in order to escape gravity? No, it could travel much more slowly, provided it had the right kind of fuel. Some of the old-fashioned fuels are too heavy. A space ship couldn't carry enough of these fuels to keep it traveling slowly until it got beyond the pull of earth's gravity. What about atomic fuel? Atomic fuel is light, but all the ordinary atomic engines would be too heavy. Inventors have had the problem of making a light space-ship engine to go with this wonderful light fuel.

What is
a satellite?

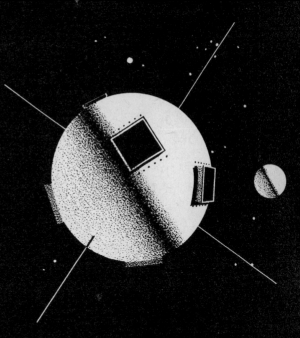

A satellite is an object that travels through space, and it always moves around and around something else that is bigger. The path a satellite follows is called its orbit. The moon travels in an orbit around the earth. It is a satellite of the earth. The earth moves in an orbit around the sun. It is one of the sun's satellites. Most orbits are oval-shaped, not perfect circles.

Men can now create new satellites. When an object shot out into space begins to circle around the sun, the moon, or the earth itself, we say that scientists have "put a satellite into orbit."

The first man-made satellite orbited around the earth. Russian scientists who put it into orbit called it a "fellow traveler" of the moon. "Sputnik" is the Russian word for fellow traveler. Soon people were calling any man-made satellite a sputnik.

9

Why don't the planets bump into each other?

The earth and all the other planets travel around the sun. Some travel faster than the earth. Some travel more slowly. Each one has its own path — its own orbit. The earth's orbit is just right for its size and speed. So are the orbits of the other planets. The sun and its family of planets all move along as regularly as clock work. Perhaps there were traffic problems long, long ago when the orbiting first started. Some scientists believe that collisions did happen. But everything moves smoothly now. You need not worry about bumping into Mars.

Can space travelers live on pills instead of food?

Just as an experiment, men have tried living on pills for a while. The pills contained dried, condensed foods — everything necessary to keep the body healthy. Scientists thought the pills might be just the thing for space travelers. But the experiment didn't last long. The men found a pill diet so unsatisfying that they began to feel cross and quarrelsome. Perhaps astronauts *could* live on pills, but they won't unless they have to.

10

What is a shooting star?

A flash of moving light suddenly appears in the sky at night. Then just as suddenly it goes out. In the old days people called it a shooting star, which was a pretty name, but not very accurate. A real star is a great glowing ball of gases thousands of miles thick. A shooting star usually weighs anywhere from a few ounces to a few pounds, and it is made of rock or metal. Scientists call it a meteor.

Thousands of meteors swarm through space, near the earth, day and night. Some of them come so close that the earth's gravity captures them and they begin to fall toward us. But the air acts as a brake and slows them down. The braked meteors get hotter, hotter — till they change to gas in a burst of glowing light. Meteors enter our atmosphere in daytime, too. Their light is too dim to be noticed in the sunlit sky. We know they are there because radar screens locate them.

2. THE ANIMAL WORLD

Why doesn't a spider get stuck in its own web?

A spider spins a web from two kinds of silky thread. One kind of silk is sticky and catches flies, moths, and other insects. The other kind of silk is not sticky and on these threads the spider runs across its web. What if the spider slips? An oily stuff on its body keeps it from getting tangled in the sticky strands.

A spider has little tubes called spinnerets on its underside. From these spinnerets comes the liquid which hardens in the air to form silk for a web.

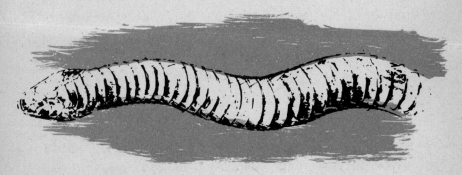

How does a snake move?

You'd find wriggling on your stomach slow work, but a snake is built for slithering. On its underside are hard scaly plates. Each plate can move. The snake lifts a plate, then pushes back with it against the earth. This backward push shoves the snake forward — the way ski poles shove a skier.

How can a fly walk on a ceiling?

A fly has a little suction cup on each of its six feet. This is how the suction cup works: It is hollow inside and slightly moist. When it is pushed against a flat surface, most of the air is squeezed out. The moisture seals the edges and keeps air from getting back in. Now there is a lot of air outside and very little inside the cup. The pressure of the outside air is strong. It holds the suction cup tightly to the ceiling.

The fly picks up three of its feet at a time to step forward. The suction cups on the other three feet hold the fly in place till their turn to move. Does this seem like a hard way to walk? It would be hard for us, but not for a fly. Flies have great strength for their size.

Why do beavers build dams?

Beavers build dams to have safe homes near a supply of food in winter. In the pond that forms behind their dam, the beavers put together a strong hut. It looks like a jumble of sticks and mud, but has a good dry room inside. The entrance is hidden under water. A beaver family — father, mother and several young ones called kits — live together in the house.

Even when the pond is frozen over, beavers usually have plenty of food. They eat the bark from tree branches and bushes which they have cut and then anchored in the mud at the bottom of the pond.

What is the smallest animal?

The very smallest creatures in the world can be seen only through a microscope. The smallest furry animal is a fat-tailed shrew, so fragile, you can break its bones by picking it up. This littlest animal is probably the biggest eater. For its size it gobbles up more food than any other four-footed creature. Every day its tiny sharp teeth chew through a pile of wood weighing two and a half times as much as it weighs. Imagine doing that yourself. If you weigh sixty pounds, you would have to eat in *one* day, 150 loaves of bread or about three pillowcases full of oatmeal.

What is the fastest animal?

The fastest *insect* is probably the botfly which darts along at forty or fifty miles an hour. Many naturalists think that the duck hawk is the fastest *bird*. Some say it can go more than 150 miles an hour. Others believe that eighty is its limit. Dolphins are fast *swimmers*. They can keep up with motorboats traveling thirty miles an hour. The cheetah, most people agree, can go faster than any other *four-legged animal*. Its record is about seventy-five miles an hour. Hunters have trained cheetahs to pursue and kill swift-running antelopes and deer.

What makes a firefly's light?

A firefly's light comes from two juices that it makes in its body. Neither kind of juice will shine all by itself, but when the two mix together with air, they glow. A firefly doesn't burn your hand if you catch it. The light is cool, like the light from a fluorescent bulb.

Scientists believe that fireflies attract their mates by flashing their lights. But no one can yet explain a strange habit of fireflies in Thailand. Large numbers of them gather in trees. Then suddenly they all light up at the same moment. On and off, on and off — sometimes several trees full of fireflies will flash in unison.

Another glowing creature is the *ferrocarril* worm that lives in South America. It has eleven pairs of little green lights along its sides and one red light on its head. If you annoy the worm it turns its lights on.

Do animals live as long as people?

Most animals have very short lives. But some live longer than people usually live. A tortoise has been known to reach the age of one hundred and fifty. Elephants grow old at just about the same rate as people. Many of them live to be sixty-five or seventy. Dogs and cats are old when they reach the age of ten, but some live longer. And one kind of insect — the seventeen-year locust — usually spends seventeen years in the earth before it comes out. Then it lives for only a few weeks.

What is the biggest animal?

The biggest creature in the world is the blue whale. If you could stretch one out across a baseball diamond with its nose on home plate, its tail would almost reach second base. A blue whale weighs as much as 150 tons, and it is very powerful. It can sink a small ship if it chooses to bash in the side with a blow of its tail. Although it lives in the sea, you musn't call it a fish. Whales are mammals. That is, they have warm blood, and the

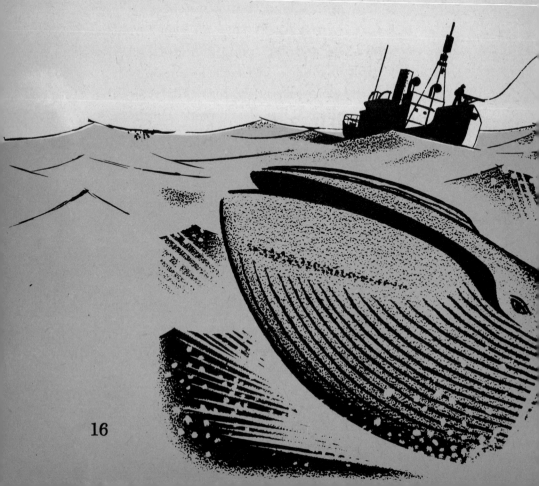

mothers feed their babies on milk from their bodies. A mother whale lies on her back in the sea while the huge baby suckles.

Is the blue whale the largest of all babies when it is first born? Yes, but there's another way of thinking about size. Suppose you compare a baby to its parents. For instance, most human mothers weigh twenty or twenty-five times as much as their new-born babies. If you think about size in this way, then the baby porcupine is the biggest. A mother porcupine weighs only three times as much as her baby when it is born.

3. HOW DOES IT WORK?

How does a thermometer work?

The thermometer on your wall is a little glass tube with a colored line inside it. The line is really a liquid called mercury that has been dyed red or blue. Since the tube is hollow, the mercury can move up and down. It stretches upward as the room gets warm and shrinks down when the room turns cold.

The marks and numbers on the tube measure the height of the mercury. If it shrinks down to the 32-mark, you will be shivering, and water will turn to ice. But when the mercury goes up as high as 90, you feel hot.

Why does the line of mercury grow taller or shorter? Like everything else, mercury is made of tiny particles called molecules. The mercury molecules are always moving, bumping into each other and bouncing away. Even when the colored line remains steady inside the tube, the molecules are shifting around and around. Heat makes them move faster. The fast-bouncing molecules shove each other farther and farther apart. So the mercury takes up more space, and it rises in the tube.

When the molecules get cold they move more slowly. Now they don't need so much bouncing space. They draw closer together, and the mercury goes down.

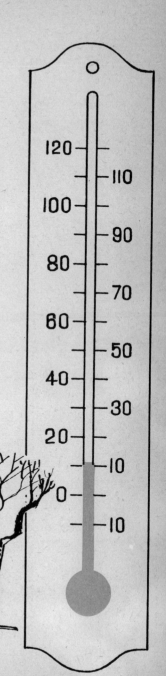

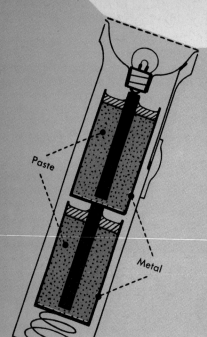

Paste

Metal

The bulb in a flashlight looks like a tiny electric light bulb. That's exactly what it is. Perhaps this seems strange. A flashlight doesn't have a wire attached to it, so it can't get electricity from the power plant. But the batteries in a flashlight *are* a kind of power plant. They send electricity through the bulb and make it glow whenever you push the button that turns it on.

How do batteries make electricity? First we have to remember that there are small particles of electricity in everything. These particles, called electrons, can be made to move from one place to another. Electrons streaming through a light bulb light it up.

Now look at the picture of a battery. The outside part is made of metal, and it has more electrons than the black rod in the middle. Between them is a kind of paste. This paste contains a chemical which can make the metal give up some of its electrons. When you turn the flashlight on, you let electrons escape from the metal. They run through the bulb and then on to the black rod. And, of course, they light the bulb on their way. From the rod they move through the paste, back to the metal again.

20

The chemical paste is something like a one-way street with a traffic cop who keeps the electrons moving from metal to bulb to rod and back to metal again.

After a battery has been used for a while the chemicals in the paste change. The movement of electrons stops, and we say the battery is dead.

What makes a ball bounce?

A rubber ball bounces because it is elastic. An elastic substance is made of molecules that do two opposite things: They give when they are pushed, but they also resist being pushed. When a ball hits the floor, the blow flattens it a little. But rubber molecules resist. They push back against the floor. And up goes the ball into the air again, as round as before. You are made of elastic material, too. Think what you would look like if the molecules in your body didn't resist when they are pushed around!

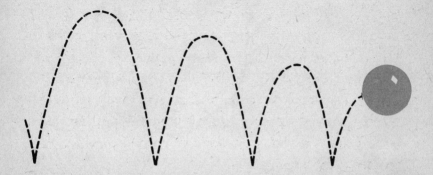

How do words travel over a telephone wire?

Perhaps you've made a tin can telephone like the one in the picture. You hold one can and a friend holds the other, with the string stretched tight between. Now let's see what happens when you talk.

First, your voice makes the air move in little waves inside the can. The sound waves strike the bottom of your tin phone and make it move in and out. This movement is called vibration. The vibration of the tin can makes the string vibrate. The vibrating string makes the bottom of the other tin can move in and out. The second tin can pushes against the air and makes sound waves. The sound waves strike your friend's ear, and he hears what you are saying.

A real telephone is something like a toy phone, but it works by electricity. Electric current runs through the wire between your house and a friend's house. The current runs steadily if nothing disturbs it. But let's see what happens when you begin to talk.

Your voice makes sound waves which hit a little round plate in the mouthpiece of the phone.

The little plate vibrates, just as the tin can did. But the plate is connected with the telephone wire in a special way. When the plate vibrates it makes the electric current wiggle unevenly.

The wiggly current travels to your friend's receiver. There it works an electric magnet. The magnet makes another little plate move in and out. This vibrating receiver plate causes sound waves which travel to your friend's ear. And so he hears what you are saying.

How does radio work?

You turn on the radio and a program comes to you from a broadcasting station miles and miles away. You know that words and music themselves haven't traveled all that distance through space, but something certainly is bringing the program from the station. What is this silent carrier of sound?

The answer is radio waves. You can't see radio waves, or feel them or even hear them. In fact, nobody knows exactly what they are. But we do know that they are made by electricity, and we have learned how to use them.

At the broadcasting station people talk or sing, instruments play, doors slam, and all of these make sound waves. The sound waves reach the microphone, and here they are changed into electricity. Then from a tall tower called the broadcasting antenna, electricity sends out radio waves. The waves travel in every direction, and some of them reach your radio antenna. Now a wonder-

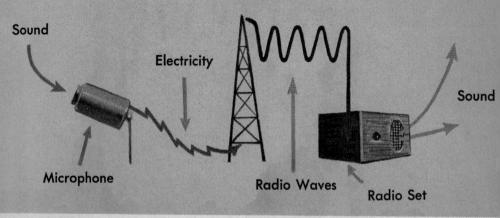

Sound

Electricity

Microphone

Radio Waves

Radio Set

Sound

ful thing happens. The radio waves start an electric current in your antenna like the one that was first made in the broadcasting station. Finally, the loudspeaker in your set changes electricity into sound, and you hear the program.

On	550	~~~~~~~	550,000	Waves
Your				Per
Dial	770	~~~~~~~	770,000	Second

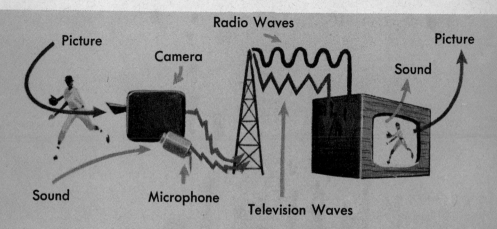

Radio Waves

Picture

Camera

Picture

Sound

Sound

Microphone

Television Waves

How does television work?

Television uses the same kind of wonderful invisible, soundless waves that make your radio work. At the broadcasting station, a special camera picks up light waves while the microphone picks up sound waves. Both are changed to electricity. Electricity makes the television waves which bring the program to your set, where it becomes sound and light to make the picture on the screen.

25

What makes a fuse burn out?

Perhaps this has happened at your house: An electric iron or a toaster or a fan gets something wrong with it — the lights suddenly go off, too. A fuse has burned out.

A fuse often seems like a nuisance, but it is really a help. Whenever something goes wrong with electricity, the wires in your house are likely to get too hot, and that may start a fire. The fuse is a guard that turns the electricity off if there is danger of fire.

If you look inside a burned fuse, you will see a little broken piece of metal. Before it was broken, electricity from the power line could run through that metal strip on its way into your house. When just the right amount ran through it, there was nothing to worry about.

Then something happened and too much electricity began to go through the strip. It got too hot, and the metal burned in two. From then on electricity couldn't run through the fuse into the house. The lights went out!

If you use too many electrical things at once, you make extra electricity run through the wire. A machine that isn't working right, or a broken cord can also make too much electricity surge through the fuse and burn it out.

Suppose the fuse wasn't there. The extra electricity would make the regular wires in your house get very hot. When they get hot enough they can start a fire. That's why you have fuses to stand guard.

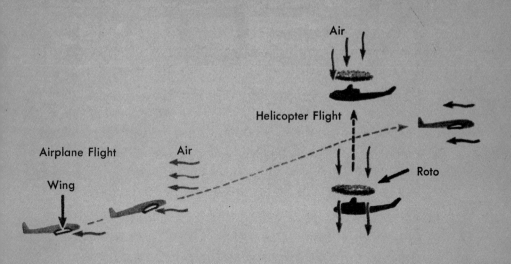

Air

Helicopter Flight

Airplane Flight

Air

Wing

Roto

How does a helicopter go straight up in the air?

A helicopter has a rotor that whirls around above the body of the machine. Actually the rotor is a wing. It lifts the helicopter just the way an airplane wing lifts the plane.

An airplane has to get up speed before it can rise off the ground. It rolls along a runway, faster and faster, until the wings are moving quickly enough for it to take off. A helicopter wing — that is, the rotor — also has to gain speed before the copter can rise. But the rotor goes faster and faster *in a circle,* while the body of the copter stays in place. Soon the whirling rotor-wing is moving quickly enough to take off. It lifts evenly, and the body of the copter follows, almost straight up.

How does a neon sign work?

A neon light is something like a fluorescent light. Neon signs are made of glass tubes shaped into words and decorations. When you push a button, the words light up — red, blue, green. The lights seems to swirl around inside the tubes. But where does it come from? There is no wire running through the tube as there is in regular electric light bulbs.

The light comes from a gas with which the tube is filled. When electricity goes through this gas, it glows very brightly. A gas called neon gives off a reddish glow, and that is where the name neon light came from. Other gases make lights that are blue or yellow. Yellow light in a blue glass tube looks green. The movement that you see in the tubes comes from the gas swirling around.

It takes very little electricity to make the neon tubes light up, and that is why they are used for huge signs.

Why does glue stick things together?

In order to see how glue works, we have to know what glue really is. Like everything else in the world, glue is made up of many tiny separate bits called molecules. Each molecule works somewhat like a magnet. It pulls the neighboring glue molecules toward it. We say it attracts them. A glue molecule also attracts the molecules of paper and wood and other materials. This attraction becomes very strong when the glue gets dry. The molecules pull hard on each other and on the materials that need to be held together, and so it makes them stick tight.

There are different kinds of glue. The molecules of some kinds attract wood or paper. Other kinds attract china or glass. Still others work well on almost all materials.

The kind of glue called mucilage is made from the hoofs and horns of animals. Model airplane "dope" is a liquid plastic. Rubber cement comes from rubber, and there is a milky white kind of glue that really is made from milk.

Why is milk pasteurized?

Milk that has been pasteurized is milk that has been heated and kept hot, but not quite boiling hot, for half an hour. Heating milk in this special way kills any germs in it that might make us sick. The word "pasteurize" comes from Pasteur, the name of the French scientist who discovered how to keep germs from spoiling food.

Why do we feel pain when we get hurt?

You fall down and bang your elbow. Immediately you know that your elbow hurts. It is as if the message had flashed to your brain: "Elbow aches!"

The message really did travel to your brain, through long, thin living threads called nerve cells. Your pain nerve cells are usually quiet. But when something bumps or scrapes them, a message goes to the brain. Your body has several million pain nerve cells. They are closer together in some places than in others. That is why a whack on the nose hurts worse than a slap on the thigh. Doctors don't know exactly how a nerve cell works when it is stimulated. They do know that chemical changes happen all along the line, and that pain signals travel to your brain at a speed of about 200 miles an hour! No wonder you yell "Ouch!" only a second after you're hurt.

Why doesn't your hair hurt when it is cut? There are no pain nerve cells in hair. The nerve cells end in the scalp. They send signals when hairs are pulled. But if hair is cut without pulling, the pain nerve cells aren't stimulated, and so cutting doesn't hurt.

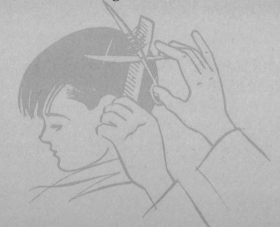

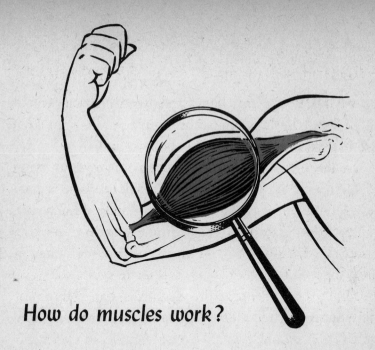

How do muscles work?

This is what a piece of muscle looks like when we put it under a magnifying glass. The long, narrow strings are called fibers. Each fiber is made of smaller bits called cells, and each cell has an unbelievably thin wall that separates it from the others. Each is filled with a soft, jelly-like material. And here comes the surprise: The cells are tiny surfaces where a slow fire burns all the time! Of course, the fire doesn't flame or glow. You can't see it. But you can feel it. Your body feels warm because its cells burn fuel.

The fuel for an automobile is gasoline, and burning gasoline makes a car run. Burning coal drives a locomotive. Food burning in the muscle cells gives us muscle power. Scientists have discovered this much. But they still don't know exactly how the wonderful cell furnaces do their part of the work of changing food into muscle power.

31

How do germs make us sick?

These germs are tiny living plants called bacteria. Like all living things they eat and grow. They can take what they need to eat from our bodies, and they grow very quickly. Each full-grown one can divide into two new bacteria. Then these two split, making four. Soon there are millions of them. All these millions of bacteria act like little factories which produce chemicals of different kinds. Some of the chemicals are poisonous. And so they make us sick.

Our bodies can manufacture chemicals, too, and some of our chemicals can kill harmful bacteria. Medicines kill others.

Another kind of germ is called a virus. Doctors still do not know exactly how a virus works, but they have invented wonderful medicines that keep some kinds of virus from harming us.

Tuberculosis   Diphtheria   Tetanus

This is the way bacteria look when they are magnified by a microscope. If you looked at a virus through the same microscope, you couldn't see it at all, because it is so tiny. Scientists must use a specially powerful instrument called an electron microscope to find out what a virus looks like.

What makes people have different colored skins?

Your color comes from chemicals in your skin. All people have these same chemicals, but not in the same amounts. Dark-skinned people have large amounts. Pinkish-white skin means that less of the color substance is present.

Scientists who study human beings do not yet know why some of us have more of the color chemicals and some have less. They *have* discovered that outside color does not make people different inside. For example, they have proved by tests that color has absolutely nothing to do with brains. Smart boys and girls are found equally among all peoples, no matter how much or how little of the color chemicals they have in their skins.

Where does our energy come from?

We can walk and run, work and play because we have energy. Our energy comes from the sun, but we don't have to be outdoors to get it. It comes to us stored up in foods. The fruits and vegetables we eat received energy from sunlight when they were growing. Our milk and eggs and meat come from animals, but *they* got their energy from plants. So our energy really does come from the sun.

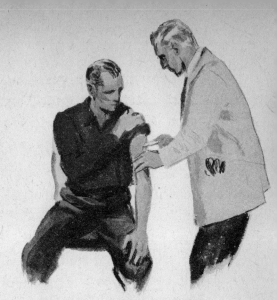

How does vaccination work?

When the doctor vaccinates you, he makes a little scratch on your skin. Then he squeezes a drop of liquid onto the scratch and rubs it in. Later the spot may feel a little sore. This one small sore spot is a sign that your whole body can now protect itself against germs which cause a disease called smallpox.

Your body fights a battle against many kinds of germs all the time. Usually it wins. That is why you stay well. Your body protects itself with various weapons. Sometimes it makes a substance that seems to paralyze the germs. Another substance dissolves them. Another makes the germs clump together so that they can't harm you.

But sometimes a strong kind of germ can take your body by surprise. It wins out for a while, and you feel sick. Your body has to work hard conquering these germs. Often, when the fight is won, that same kind of germ can not make you sick again.

Now suppose your body could have practice in winning battles. Suppose it could fight some weak germs before it had to battle against strong ones of the same kind. Would this give it the power to conquer the strong ones before they could make you sick? The answer is yes. That is what happens when you get vaccinated. Weak germs floating in liquid enter your body through the scratch the doctor makes. These weak germs give your body practice in making a weapon to use against strong smallpox germs. If the smallpox germs enter your body later on, they cannot make you sick.

How do we know what's good for us to eat?

Long ago a French explorer named Cartier spent a winter on a ship that was frozen tight in ice of the St. Lawrence River. He had plenty of food aboard, yet many of his men grew sick. An Indian chief told Cartier the sailors would be cured if they drank tea made from the needles of a certain evergreen tree. The tea cured the men. Later, English sailors on long voyages had the same disease. They discovered that the juice of limes would cure it. Both the limes and the evergreen contain a vitamin which is found in fresh foods. The sailors got sick because they had no fresh fruit or vegetables.

People all over the world have learned by trial and error which foods they must have in order to keep alive. But nowadays food scientists do better than that. They study people and animals. They experiment with foods and chemicals. They are finding out what the needs of our bodies are and which foods best fill these needs.

What makes popcorn pop?

Steam makes popcorn pop. But everybody knows popcorn isn't wet. Then where does the steam come from? It comes from *inside* each grain of corn.

Before you put a grain of corn in a popper it feels very dry. But inside each grain are tiny invisible drops of water. It's as if each droplet were wrapped in a little white "coat" that holds it tight.

When a grain of corn gets hot in the popper, the drops of water get hot, too. Soon the water turns to steam. Then pop! The steam bursts out, leaving a fluffy pile of popped corn.

What makes soda pop fizz?

The bubbly stuff in soda pop is a gas, but not the same kind of gas that burns in your kitchen stove.

As long as a bottle of pop isn't moved, the gas remains mixed with the flavored water. But if the bottle is jiggled, tiny bubbles of gas start to rise. These bubbles are lighter than the water, so they float to the top. When you take the cap off the bottle, the bubbles keep on rising. More bubbles follow. They come out so fast that they bring some of the pop along with them in a frothy foam. As all these bubbles burst they make a fizzing sound.

What makes iron get rusty?

You leave your roller skates out in the rain. Next day they have reddish orange spots on them. What has happened? What made them rusty?

Air and rain rusted the iron. Air has oxygen in it, and here is the interesting thing: When oxygen and water and iron come together something happens. The three substances join and produce an entirely new one — rust. We say that air, water and iron have combined and that a chemical change has taken place.

Iron things don't get rusty if they are covered by something that keeps out oxygen and water. Grease or oil will do. Oil forms a thin coat that protects your skates. Paint protects iron fences, bridges and ships.

Silver turns black for almost the same reason that iron gets rusty. Gases in the air or chemicals in food combine with the silver and make a new substance that we call tarnish. Tarnish sticks so tight that we use silver polish to clean it off.

Why do trees lose their leaves in fall?

All spring and summer the leaves on a tree do an important job. They act like little food factories manufacturing food for the living tree. To do this they need air and water, sunshine and minerals from the soil.

Water comes to the leaves up the tree trunk from the roots. Roots get water from soil around them. Leaves breathe air in and out through tiny holes that you can see only with a microscope. When they breathe out, they give off invisible droplets of water at the same time.

All summer long the little leaf-factories work at making food for the tree. But in fall, when there is less sunlight, they stop. The tree has already stored up enough food to last through the winter. Now it rests — the way a bear rests when it goes to sleep in a hollow log or a cave after cold weather comes.

Just before the tree starts to rest it corks up all the little holes at the base of the leaves through which water has been coming. It makes a bit of real cork, and this tough waterproof stuff actually pushes each leaf off as it grows. The leaves fall, and that's why we often call autumn "the fall."

If trees didn't cork up the water tubes, the leaves would keep on breathing out water, even after the ground was frozen. But roots can't take water out of frozen ground. And so, if water kept disappearing, the inside of the tree would dry out and it would die.

What makes the colors in a rainbow?

Be a detective the next time you see a rainbow. Look for clues that will tell you what causes it. Clue number one: It is daytime. You have never seen a rainbow at night. There aren't any rainbows after dark. They appear only when there is sunlight. Sunlight may be the thing that causes a rainbow's colors.

Clue number two: You don't see a rainbow until there has been rain somewhere. Perhaps you're standing in a dry spot, and the shower has been elsewhere. But rain is involved, as well as sunlight.

Now let's examine the first clue — sunlight. Scientists have noticed what happens to sunlight when it passes through a special kind of glass. They have found that yellowish white sunlight really has all the different colors scrambled together in it.

Is there anything in the sky that can unscramble the colors in sunlight? Can raindrops do the trick? Yes. When sunlight passes through raindrops in just the right way, the light is broken up into many colors and spread out in the sky.

Rainbow colors give a clue to another question: What makes the sky blue? Sunlight's colors can be unscrambled by dust in the air, by gases, by the air itself. These things break light up, and they stop all of the colors except blue. But the blue light bounces away and reaches our eyes. And so the sky looks blue. Of course, only a part of the sun's light is stopped in the sky. The rest of it reaches us still looking yellow-white.

4. EARTH AND SKY

What makes an echo?

People used to think an echo was made by a kind of fairy who lived in the rocks. When a person shouted something, the echo fairy shouted it right back. Of course, you know that an echo is really the sound of your own voice. You simply hear the sound twice. The sound travels through the air like any other sound. It goes in waves. If you could see the waves, they would look very much like the ripples you make when you drop a pebble into a pool of water. Sound waves travel through the air in every direction.

Suppose you stand in front of a cliff and call out "Hello!" Some of the sound waves hit your ears immediately. Others strike the smooth, hard surface of the cliff, and then they come bouncing back. We say they are reflected. A moment later, these reflected waves reach your ears. And that is how you hear an echo.

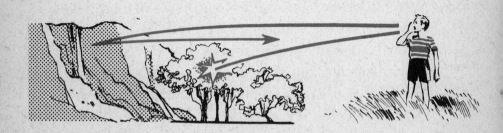

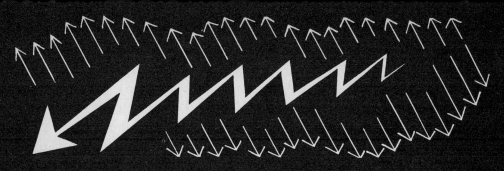

What makes thunder?

Lightning is the cause of thunder! As lightning jumps across the sky, it heats the air. The air grows hot so suddenly that it gives a terrific push outward. This leaves an almost empty space along the lightning's path. Cold air rushes in to fill the space. Air from one side bumps into air from every other side. The bumping makes the tremendous noise. Thunder rolls and surges and rumbles. That is because the lightning jumps in uneven flashes. Sometimes thunder has extra rumbles. These are echoes that come from hills and valleys and from the clouds themselves.

Why do we see the lightning before we hear thunder?

Light travels very fast, 186,000 miles in one second. That is seven times the distance around the world in the time it takes you to say your name. But sound travels more slowly. In one second it goes only about a fifth of a mile. That is about the length of four city blocks. Since light travels faster than sound, we usually *see* lightning before we *hear* thunder. Only if the lightning strikes near you do you sense both at almost the same instant.

41

How do we know what it's like inside the earth?

Suppose you could dig a hole four thousand miles deep, straight to the center of the earth. What would you find on the way? Although the deepest oil well goes down only about four miles, scientists know a great deal about what the earth is like farther down.

First comes a crust of ordinary rock. This is twenty or thirty miles thick in most places. Under the Pacific Ocean this crust is only a few miles thick.

Next comes a layer of heavier rock about 1,800 miles thick. Inside this layer is the earth's core. The core seems to be a sort of liquid metal, very hot and much heavier than any metals you have ever seen.

Information about the inside of the earth comes from an instrument called the seismograph. Every time there is an earthquake anywhere in the world, a seismograph makes a wavy line on special paper. Scientists study these wavy lines to find out when and where the earth is quaking. But they can also study the lines to find out what kind of rock lies deep in the earth.

Will we ever have a look at the earth's core itself? Probably not. But some day we will certainly understand better what it is made of.

Scientists hope to get a sample of the rock between the earth's crust and core. They plan to drill a deep hole in the floor of the Pacific Ocean using machinery like this.

Is the world getting warmer?

Perhaps you've heard somebody's grandmother say, "Winters aren't as cold as they used to be when I was a girl." Scientists are beginning to think Grandma is right, if she lives in the northeastern part of the United States. That part of the world is warmer than it was fifty years ago. But along the Pacific coast the weather seems to have grown a little colder. Alaska is warming up, and glaciers are melting in other parts of the world. Why? Scientists have made many guesses, but they admit they don't really know. At any rate, if all the ice in the world melted, the oceans would rise at least 200 feet.

How near is the nearest star?

Our sun is really a star, and it is closer to us than any other. Beyond the sun, the star nearest us is more than 25 trillion miles away.

Distances in space are so great that astronomers measure distance by light years. A light year is the number of miles that light can travel in a year. Light travels about 186,000 miles a second.

The light you see when you look at the nearest star has been traveling for almost four and a half years! If you are in the fourth grade, the light that you see now left that star when you were still in kindergarten. It has been speeding toward the earth, night and day, ever since then.

How do volcanoes get started?

At certain places under the hard rock crust of the earth there are pools of hot *liquid* rock. Perhaps radioactivity has heated these places so that the rock is molten. Experts aren't sure about this, but they know that the hot liquid rock moves toward the surface through any cracks or weak places in the solid rock above it. It even dissolves hard rock, making weak places through which to push.

In one way or another it manages to get out onto the surface, and we call it lava. Lava may break free suddenly with a tremendous explosion. Or it may flow out of a big crack. When it does this it looks and acts somewhat like honey.

A volcano is formed when hot lava escapes from the earth.

Some volcanoes shoot "ash" into the air. As this volcanic ash falls back to earth it builds up a cone-shaped mountain around the hole out of which it comes. One day in 1943 a farmer in Mexico saw smoke coming from a three-inch hole that had suddenly appeared in his cornfield. The hole grew and began to spew out volcanic ash. In a week the ash had built up a cone 500 feet high. A few weeks later it was 1000 feet high and still growing. A new volcano had been born.

The ash out of which the volcano grew was not real ash. It was lava that had been sprayed up into the air where it cooled and hardened. But it only cooled *after* it had gotten hotter than it was down inside the earth.

Lava

Ash & Cinders

EARTH'S CRUST

Varies Many
Tens of Miles

LIQUID ROCK

Lava grows hotter when it mixes with oxygen. The same thing happens when it touches water. Some volcanoes, erupting under water at the bottom of the ocean, keep building themselves up until they become islands. Hawaii is a group of volcanic islands.

A mountain called Vesuvius in Italy suddenly exploded nearly 2,000 years ago. Deadly gases poured down over the neighboring city of Pompeii and killed almost all the people there. Then volcanic ash settled over everything, burying the city. By digging up Pompeii scientists have learned a great deal about how people looked and lived in the ancient world.

What makes the waves in the ocean?

You can make little waves by blowing hard into a bowl of water. Ocean waves are just the same, only bigger, and the blowing of the wind causes them. Perhaps you have seen waves on a perfectly still day. These waves started far away. Somewhere over the ocean wind pushed against the water and set it into motion. Ripples formed and grew into bigger ripples and finally into waves. The power of wind on water is very great. Waves can travel five thousand miles and more beyond the place where a wind starts them. Some waves are also formed when the tides go in and out.

Sometimes an earthquake or a volcano at the bottom of the sea causes waves. Enormous waves caused by earthquakes are called tidal waves.

Why is the ocean salty?

Salt comes from rocks. It has to be loosened from solid rock and washed down to the ocean. Heat and cold, freezing and thawing, make cracks in the rocks, and rain washes the salt out.

Long ago, when the world was very new, sea water probably tasted just like water from your faucet. But rain has been washing the rocks for millions and millions of years, and gradually the oceans have grown more and more salty. Every year rivers carry several billion tons of salt, dissolved in water, down to the sea.

Is there gold in the sea?

The sea has more gold than any mine in the world. There is ninety million dollars' worth of gold in every cubic mile of sea water. (You can imagine a cubic mile of water if you think of filling a tank a mile wide, a mile long, and a mile deep.) The cost of separating the gold from the water is much greater than the gold itself is worth. So it's much more sensible to fish in the ocean for good things to eat!

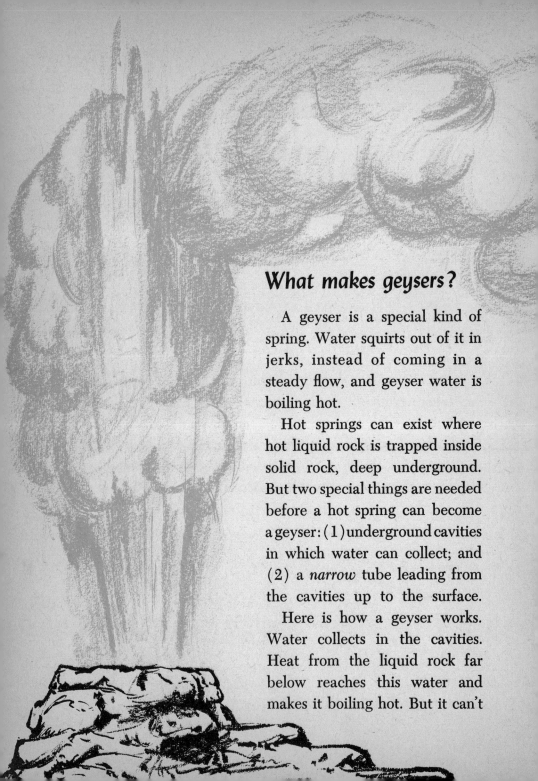

What makes geysers?

A geyser is a special kind of spring. Water squirts out of it in jerks, instead of coming in a steady flow, and geyser water is boiling hot.

Hot springs can exist where hot liquid rock is trapped inside solid rock, deep underground. But two special things are needed before a hot spring can become a geyser: (1) underground cavities in which water can collect; and (2) a *narrow* tube leading from the cavities up to the surface.

Here is how a geyser works. Water collects in the cavities. Heat from the liquid rock far below reaches this water and makes it boiling hot. But it can't behave the way ordinary boiling water behaves in a pan on the stove. In the pan, boiling hot water turns to steam; the steam rises from the bottom, and flies off into the air. But the hot water in the geyser cavity can't escape so easily. Remember, there is only a long narrow tube leading to the air outside. The cold water in it acts somewhat like a huge cork in a bottle. The steam can't escape because of the cork. The temperature of the water goes up and up. Still it can't let off steam. Gradually tremendous pressure builds up way down inside the cavity.

Then at last something has to give. Steam presses so hard that water rises through the narrow peak of the geyser and spills over. With this water gone, more water down below turns to steam like a flash. It, too, is pushed out.

Faster and faster, water changes to steam. More and more water is forced up the narrow tube. It rises in a solid column, higher and higher into the air. Then everything stops as suddenly as it began. The cavities down below are empty. They must fill up before the geyser spouts again.

Old Faithful is the name of a famous geyser in Yellowstone National Park. It can be counted on to spout once every sixty-five minutes.

What set the sun on fire?

How did the sun begin in the first place? All of space seems to be filled with a very thin gas. This gas is not spread evenly. At places it is thicker than at others. Here and there it is thick enough to contain solid or liquid particles and to look like a cloud. Apparently light from the stars pushes this thin gas around, and it keeps on pushing when it has formed a cloud. The cloud develops into a kind of whirlwind — or a whirling collection of whirlwinds.

Something like that happened about six billion years ago to one huge dust cloud which became our sun. Its particles and gases crowded closer and closer together. They squeezed and crowded together so hard that the pressure began to create heat. Finally the heat turned one of the gases called hydrogen into another gas called helium. This is just what happens when an

H-bomb explodes. The sun had become a gigantic H-bomb!

Now there was a tremendous increase in heat and light. Scientists estimate that the sun has enough hydrogen in it to keep going at the present rate for a very, very long time. But at last the sun will have changed so much that a new thing will happen. It will suddenly get even hotter. The heat will be so tremendous that it will burn up everything on earth and boil away the seas.

This flare-up will last only a short time, and then the sun will suddenly shrivel and grow cold and dark.

You don't have to worry about all this. Experts say that the sun's final burst won't happen until about six billion years from now.

What is the sun made of?

The sun is a ball of gas so fiery that it glows with a bright light. Most of the gas in the sun is hydrogen. Some of it is helium. The sun also contains many of the other substances that we have here on earth — for example, iron and nickel. On earth these metals are solid, the way ice is solid. You know what happens when ice is heated. It turns to water and finally to a hot gas that we call steam. The sun is so hot that the metals in it are not solid or even liquid. They are gases instead!

What makes lightning?

Lightning is really electricity—lots of electricity that jumps through the air in huge sparks.

You can make little jumping sparks of electricity if you rub a cat's fur or comb your hair with a hard rubber comb. Probably the giant sparks of lightning are caused in somewhat the same way.

Lightning sparks start in the clouds. Great winds blow through a rain cloud and whip the raindrops around and tear some of them apart. Tremendous action goes on, and this action electrifies the cloud. Weathermen don't know exactly how it happens, but great charges of electricity build up. Suddenly there comes a flash. The lightning jumps from one part of the cloud to another. Or it leaps between the cloud and the earth.

Lightning usually seems like one enormous quivering spark, but it is really several sparks. It travels in a zigzag path, and that is what gives it a jagged look.

Is lightning dangerous?

Yes, lightning can be dangerous. If you are outdoors and see lightning you should go into a house for protection. In the old days people shut their windows to keep the lightning out. They thought it could blow in with the wind. But of course it can't.

Lightning often strikes trees. So you should never stay under a tree during a thunderstorm.

An automobile is a safe place, and so is a cave. Lightning often strikes water so you shouldn't swim during a thunderstorm.

Here is a way to tell whether lightning is close. Start to count the instant you see the flash. Count until you hear the thunder: One-and-two-and-three-and-four-and-five-and. If you can count to five in this way, before you hear the thunder, the lightning has struck about a mile away, and it can't possibly do you any harm. If you can count to ten, it is two miles away. When lightning is really close, you see the flash and hear the thunder at almost the same moment.

If you could stretch electric cords from the ground to the clouds, there wouldn't be any lightning. The electricity would run through the cords into the earth. Of course, we can't plug cords into the clouds. But people often do have metal lightning rods that stick up above houses and barns. The electricity jumps from the cloud to the rod. Instead of hitting the building, it runs into the earth.

5. LONG AGO...

What is a fossil?

Did you ever break a stone in two and find something inside that looks like a picture of a fern or a clam or a fish or a bug? We call these things fossils, and they are more than pictures. They are the real shapes of real plants and animals that lived on earth long, long ago.

How could a plant or animal get inside a hard piece of rock? This is the story of one fossil fish: Millions of years ago it died and fell into the mud at the bottom of the lake. A river brought more mud down from the mountains and dumped it on top of the fish. At last the river had piled up many layers of mud and sand, one on top of the other. By now the fish's body was no longer the same as it had been. Minerals from the water had taken the place of flesh and bone. But nothing disturbed the spot where it lay, and so its shape stayed there, molded in the mud.

After a long time, the mud began to harden. It turned to stone. Then came great changes in the earth's surface. The ground under the lake heaved and moved upward. The rock with our fish in it was pushed up, high and dry. And there it stayed till we found it.

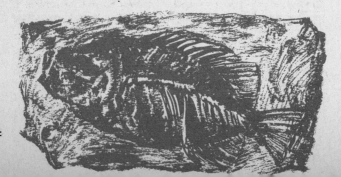

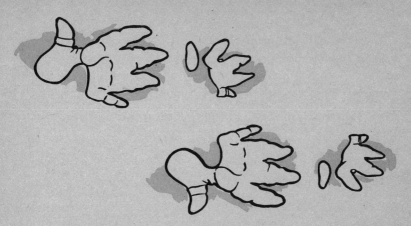

These fossil footprints had scientists fooled for almost a hundred years. They look as if they had been made by an animal that crossed its feet with every step it took! Finally someone figured out that the animal had a little toe that resembled a thumb. It was probably a relative of the dinosaurs. (After Peabody.)

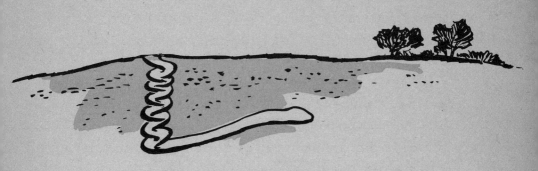

The rocks hold many kinds of fossils. Besides plants and animals themselves, you can sometimes find burrows where animals lived. The one in the picture is called a "devil's corkscrew," and it was probably the home of a prehistoric beaver. Fossil worm tracks and dinosaur footprints are often found. (After G. G. Simpson.)

How do we know about prehistoric animals?

Many strange animals used to live in the world. Long, long ago there were huge flying monsters with leathery wings but no feathers. At another time horses were about the size of dogs. Animals resembling elephants had long woolly hair. These and thousands of other ancient animals have all disappeared. How do we know that they ever lived?

Luckily some of them have been preserved in ice. Woolly elephant-like mammoths got frozen into quicksand in Alaska and Siberia at least ten thousand years ago. The cold kept them perfectly, and from time to time people still find them and dig them out of their natural deep-freeze.

In California something different happened. Many ancient animals fell into a lake of black, sticky tar. The tar was antiseptic, and so the animals' bodies were preserved.

In other places sand or mud covered animals when they died. Their bodies decayed but their bones didn't. Gradually the sand or mud turned to stone. Now, millions of years later, scientists can study the bones preserved in stone. By good detective work they can figure out from the skeltons what the whole bodies must have looked like, thousands or millions of years ago.

Dinosaur National Monument is a place where a great many dinosaurs lived and died about 140 million years ago. Scientists have dug up lots of bones there, and they have cut away one side of a hill, leaving other bones in place, so that visitors can see what the remains of a prehistoric animal look like when it is being discovered.

Did cave men make caves?

Prehistoric men *found* the caves they lived in; they didn't have to make them. Most of these natural caves were made by water eating holes in rock underground.

How can water eat rock? It must be rock of a special kind, like limestone. And the water must contain an acid that eats away at stone. Ordinary rain water has acid in it!

This is how limestone caves were formed. Water seeped down from the surface, found tiny holes and cracks in the rock, and filled them up. Gradually the acid in the water ate away the rock and made the holes larger. This took thousands of years, because the amount of acid in the water was very small. Ever so slowly the holes grew until some of them were enormous. Now there was a cave underground, completely filled with water. Then changes took place in the earth, and all the water drained out. The cave was filled with air.

Why did dinosaurs disappear from the earth?

What happened to the dinosaurs? Why did they all die? This is a puzzle that hasn't been solved. Many scientists believe that the huge creatures disappeared because the climate changed. The warm swampy lands where they lived grew dry and chilly. They couldn't find enough to eat because water plants began to disappear. They grew weak from hunger, and when cold weather came they suffered even more because they were so big they couldn't crawl into caves or holes for shelter. Gradually the dinosaurs all starved to death or died of the cold.

Probably no one will ever find out exactly what

happened. But scientists agree on one main idea: The world around the dinosaurs changed. The animals themselves didn't. They couldn't make themselves change to fit their new world. And so they died out.

How did people learn to talk?

Human beings have special muscles in their tongues. No other animals have these muscles. Tongue muscles are controlled by one particular part of the brain, and this part is bigger in human beings than in any other animal. The result of these two facts is that people can make more different kinds of sound than any other creatures can make. Of course, babies aren't born knowing how to make sense with all these sounds. They must learn to talk. And language had to be invented first.

Maybe the first words anyone spoke were imitations of the sounds people heard around them — sounds like *buzz, pop, snap.* Most likely people started to talk because they felt they just *had* to say things to each other. Nobody really knows how talking began, but all it needed was a start. A few people agreed that a few sounds would have certain meanings, and then they could use these first words to help make others. The fashion of talking spread rapidly. Possibly speech was invented several different times in several different parts of the world. At any rate, there are about 3,000 different languages spoken on earth today.

How could people build the pyramids without big machines?

Long, long ago, before cranes or elevators were invented, the kings of Egypt had great tombs built for themselves. These tombs, the pyramids, were made of enormous stone blocks. Unless you know the trick, it seems impossible for men without big machines to stack the blocks up one on top of the other.

This is what the pyramid builders did: They set the bottom layer of stones in place. Then they built a gently sloping road that led up onto this first layer. Next they hauled more stones, one by one, up the sloping road and set a second layer in place. Again they dragged stones up the slope to build the third layer. And so, over and over, they raised the road for each row of stones. When the last block was in place, they cleared the road completely away.

The Egyptians used no wagons or animals to haul their stones. They had only human muscle-power and wooden rollers. Men, pulling on ropes attached to wooden platforms, rolled the heavy loads across the

60

desert and up the slopes. The Great Pyramid, built 4,500 years ago, is nearly 500 feet high, and it took about 100,000 people altogether to do the work. The king paid them in onions, radishes and garlic!

What was the first language that people spoke?

Nobody knows what the first language was. But scientists feel quite sure that nobody speaks it today, because all languages change and keep on changing as long as people use them. One language may change in different ways in different places and grow into several separate languages.

Children don't always use words exactly the way their parents do. They make small changes in the sounds or in the meaning. In time these little changes add up to big changes. If we could meet the people who spoke English five hundred years ago, we probably couldn't understand much of what they said.

People keep inventing words. For example, *radium* became the name for a new radioactive substance when scientists discovered it less than sixty years ago.

English itself is a mixture of several languages. Scientists believe that these languages and many others all grew out of the same ancestor language which they call Indo-European. Nobody speaks Indo-European now. But some of its descendants, are English, German, Latin, French, Greek, Russian and many of the different tongues spoken in India.

What is a mummy?

A mummy is a dead animal or human being whose body has been preserved. The skin looks as if it had changed to leather, and it lasts for hundreds or even thousands of years.

Long, long ago in ancient Egypt someone discovered the secret of using oils and spices and chemicals to preserve flesh. Mummy-making became part of the Egyptian religion. The bodies of dead kings and queens were carefully prepared and then stored away in beautiful boxes in secret tombs. Many of the tombs have now been found, and thanks to the person who invented the strange

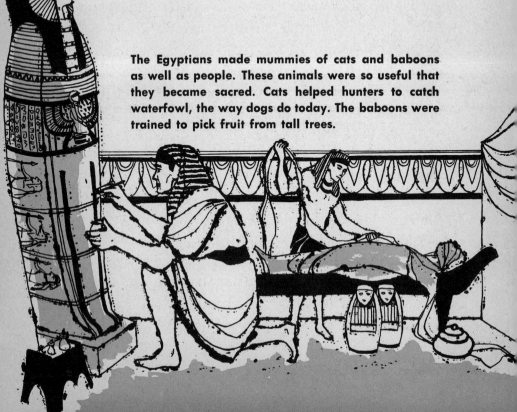

The Egyptians made mummies of cats and baboons as well as people. These animals were so useful that they became sacred. Cats helped hunters to catch waterfowl, the way dogs do today. The baboons were trained to pick fruit from tall trees.

custom of making mummies. we know what the Egyptians looked like so long ago.

In our own Southwest the bodies of ancient people were also preserved, but in a different way. There the climate was so dry that the flesh grew leathery after death without any special treatment. Archeologists have found mummies wrapped in turkey-feather blankets and stored in the closed rooms of houses. They have discovered others buried in the earth where moisture couldn't reach them. Thanks only to the dry air of the Southwest, we know what the ancestors of present-day Indians looked like.

How did the universe get started?

Many scientists believe that there was always a universe and that there always will be a universe. In other words, it didn't get started. It has always been there. But particular stars and planets and shooting stars have not always been the way they are now. Each of them did have a beginning. Each of them has changed a great deal since that beginning. Old stars are always fading out and shriveling up. Shooting stars are always coming to a sudden end when they bump into some larger body in space. And somewhere in the universe new stars are always being formed.

How did anybody ever figure out all the answers in this book?

No one person figured out the answers to all these questions. It took millions of people thousands of years to discover the facts and put them together. But you can learn these facts in a day or two. You can do so because part of your body specializes in learning — your *brain*.

Your brain can store up information and rearrange it and put it together in new combinations. You can invent things entirely inside your head. Then your brain can test an invention to see whether or not it works.

How can a brain do that? Scientists don't really know. They have made experiments with rats, and they have discovered something interesting about chemicals in the animals' brains. They tested rats that had learned to find the way along a complicated path called a maze. They also tested rats that had not learned to go through the maze. More of a certain chemical appeared in the brains of the rats who had learned the trick!

Was the chemical caused by the learning? Or did the chemical have to be in the brain before learning could begin? Does the same chemical behave in the same way in people's brains? Will scientists ever discover how the brain works?

Maybe someday, by using *your* brain, you will help to find the answers.